ADDRESS BOOK
GREEN

The Pocket Size Address Book

www.journalsrus.com

Table of Content

Name	Page		Name	Page

THIS PAGE WAS
INTENTIONALLY
LEFT BLANK

NAME..

ADDRESS...

....

MOBILE # (Cell)...

HOME #..

WORK #...

FAX...

EMAIL...

NAME..

ADDRESS...

....

MOBILE # (Cell)...

HOME #..

WORK #...

FAX...

EMAIL...

NAME..

ADDRESS...

....

MOBILE # (Cell)...

HOME #..

WORK #...

FAX...

EMAIL...

NOTES:

NAME...

ADDRESS...

....

MOBILE # (Cell)...

HOME #...

WORK #..

FAX...

EMAIL..

NAME...

ADDRESS...

....

MOBILE # (Cell)...

HOME #...

WORK #..

FAX...

EMAIL..

NAME...

ADDRESS...

....

MOBILE # (Cell)...

HOME #...

WORK #..

FAX...

EMAIL..

NOTES:

NAME..

ADDRESS...

....

MOBILE # (Cell)...

HOME #...

WORK #...

FAX...

EMAIL..

NAME..

ADDRESS...

....

MOBILE # (Cell)...

HOME #...

WORK #...

FAX...

EMAIL..

NAME..

ADDRESS...

....

MOBILE # (Cell)...

HOME #...

WORK #...

FAX...

EMAIL..

NOTES:

NAME..
ADDRESS...
....
MOBILE # (Cell)...
HOME #...
WORK #..
FAX..
EMAIL...

NAME..
ADDRESS...
....
MOBILE # (Cell)...
HOME #...
WORK #..
FAX..
EMAIL...

NAME..
ADDRESS...
....
MOBILE # (Cell)...
HOME #...
WORK #..
FAX..
EMAIL...

NOTES:

NAME..

ADDRESS..

....

MOBILE # (Cell)..

HOME #...

WORK #...

FAX...

EMAIL..

NAME..

ADDRESS..

....

MOBILE # (Cell)..

HOME #...

WORK #...

FAX...

EMAIL..

NAME..

ADDRESS..

....

MOBILE # (Cell)..

HOME #...

WORK #...

FAX...

EMAIL..

NOTES:

NAME...

ADDRESS..

....

MOBILE # (Cell)..

HOME #...

WORK #...

FAX...

EMAIL..

NAME...

ADDRESS..

....

MOBILE # (Cell)..

HOME #...

WORK #...

FAX...

EMAIL..

NAME...

ADDRESS..

....

MOBILE # (Cell)..

HOME #...

WORK #...

FAX...

EMAIL..

NOTES:

NAME...

ADDRESS...

....

MOBILE # (Cell)...

HOME #...

WORK #...

FAX..

EMAIL...

NAME...

ADDRESS...

....

MOBILE # (Cell)...

HOME #...

WORK #...

FAX..

EMAIL...

NAME...

ADDRESS...

....

MOBILE # (Cell)...

HOME #...

WORK #...

FAX..

EMAIL...

NOTES:

NAME...

ADDRESS...

....

MOBILE # (Cell)...

HOME #..

WORK #...

FAX...

EMAIL..

NAME...

ADDRESS...

....

MOBILE # (Cell)...

HOME #..

WORK #...

FAX...

EMAIL..

NAME...

ADDRESS...

....

MOBILE # (Cell)...

HOME #..

WORK #...

FAX...

EMAIL..

NOTES:

NAME..

ADDRESS..

....

MOBILE # (Cell)..

HOME #...

WORK #..

FAX...

EMAIL...

NAME..

ADDRESS..

....

MOBILE # (Cell)..

HOME #...

WORK #..

FAX...

EMAIL...

NAME..

ADDRESS..

....

MOBILE # (Cell)..

HOME #...

WORK #..

FAX...

EMAIL...

NOTES:

NAME..
ADDRESS..
....
MOBILE # (Cell)..
HOME #...
WORK #...
FAX..
EMAIL..

NAME..
ADDRESS..
....
MOBILE # (Cell)..
HOME #...
WORK #...
FAX..
EMAIL..

NAME..
ADDRESS..
....
MOBILE # (Cell)..
HOME #...
WORK #...
FAX..
EMAIL..

NOTES:

NAME..

ADDRESS...

....

MOBILE # (Cell)..

HOME #...

WORK #..

FAX..

EMAIL...

NAME..

ADDRESS...

....

MOBILE # (Cell)..

HOME #...

WORK #..

FAX..

EMAIL...

NAME..

ADDRESS...

....

MOBILE # (Cell)..

HOME #...

WORK #..

FAX..

EMAIL...

NOTES:

NAME..

ADDRESS..

....

MOBILE # (Cell)..

HOME #..

WORK #..

FAX..

EMAIL..

NAME..

ADDRESS..

....

MOBILE # (Cell)..

HOME #..

WORK #..

FAX..

EMAIL..

NAME..

ADDRESS..

....

MOBILE # (Cell)..

HOME #..

WORK #..

FAX..

EMAIL..

NOTES:

NAME...
ADDRESS...
....
MOBILE # (Cell)...
HOME #..
WORK #..
FAX..
EMAIL..

NAME...
ADDRESS...
....
MOBILE # (Cell)...
HOME #..
WORK #..
FAX..
EMAIL..

NAME...
ADDRESS...
....
MOBILE # (Cell)...
HOME #..
WORK #..
FAX..
EMAIL..

NOTES:

NAME..

ADDRESS...

....

MOBILE # (Cell)...

HOME #...

WORK #...

FAX..

EMAIL...

NAME..

ADDRESS...

....

MOBILE # (Cell)...

HOME #...

WORK #...

FAX..

EMAIL...

NAME..

ADDRESS...

....

MOBILE # (Cell)...

HOME #...

WORK #...

FAX..

EMAIL...

NOTES:

NAME..
ADDRESS..
....
MOBILE # (Cell)...
HOME #..
WORK #..
FAX...
EMAIL...

NAME..
ADDRESS..
....
MOBILE # (Cell)...
HOME #..
WORK #..
FAX...
EMAIL...

NAME..
ADDRESS..
....
MOBILE # (Cell)...
HOME #..
WORK #..
FAX...
EMAIL...

NOTES:

NAME...
ADDRESS...
....
MOBILE # (Cell)..
HOME #...
WORK #...
FAX...
EMAIL...

NAME...
ADDRESS...
....
MOBILE # (Cell)..
HOME #...
WORK #...
FAX...
EMAIL...

NAME...
ADDRESS...
....
MOBILE # (Cell)..
HOME #...
WORK #...
FAX...
EMAIL...

NOTES:

NAME...

ADDRESS...

....

MOBILE # (Cell)...

HOME #...

WORK #...

FAX...

EMAIL...

NAME...

ADDRESS...

....

MOBILE # (Cell)...

HOME #...

WORK #...

FAX...

EMAIL...

NAME...

ADDRESS...

....

MOBILE # (Cell)...

HOME #...

WORK #...

FAX...

EMAIL...

NOTES:

NAME...

ADDRESS..

....

MOBILE # (Cell)..

HOME #..

WORK #..

FAX..

EMAIL...

NAME...

ADDRESS..

....

MOBILE # (Cell)..

HOME #..

WORK #..

FAX..

EMAIL...

NAME...

ADDRESS..

....

MOBILE # (Cell)..

HOME #..

WORK #..

FAX..

EMAIL...

<u>NOTES:</u>

NAME...
ADDRESS...
....
MOBILE # (Cell)..
HOME #...
WORK #...
FAX...
EMAIL...

NAME...
ADDRESS...
....
MOBILE # (Cell)..
HOME #...
WORK #...
FAX...
EMAIL...

NAME...
ADDRESS...
....
MOBILE # (Cell)..
HOME #...
WORK #...
FAX...
EMAIL...

NOTES:

NAME..

ADDRESS...

....

MOBILE # (Cell)...

HOME #...

WORK #...

FAX..

EMAIL..

NAME..

ADDRESS...

....

MOBILE # (Cell)...

HOME #...

WORK #...

FAX..

EMAIL..

NAME..

ADDRESS...

....

MOBILE # (Cell)...

HOME #...

WORK #...

FAX..

EMAIL..

NOTES:

NAME..

ADDRESS..

....

MOBILE # (Cell)..

HOME #..

WORK #...

FAX..

EMAIL...

NAME..

ADDRESS..

....

MOBILE # (Cell)..

HOME #..

WORK #...

FAX..

EMAIL...

NAME..

ADDRESS..

....

MOBILE # (Cell)..

HOME #..

WORK #...

FAX..

EMAIL...

NOTES:

NAME..

ADDRESS..

....

MOBILE # (Cell)..

HOME #..

WORK #..

FAX..

EMAIL..

NAME..

ADDRESS..

....

MOBILE # (Cell)..

HOME #..

WORK #..

FAX..

EMAIL..

NAME..

ADDRESS..

....

MOBILE # (Cell)..

HOME #..

WORK #..

FAX..

EMAIL..

NOTES:

NAME...

ADDRESS...

....

MOBILE # (Cell)..

HOME #..

WORK #...

FAX..

EMAIL..

NAME...

ADDRESS...

....

MOBILE # (Cell)..

HOME #..

WORK #...

FAX..

EMAIL..

NAME...

ADDRESS...

....

MOBILE # (Cell)..

HOME #..

WORK #...

FAX..

EMAIL..

NOTES:

NAME..

ADDRESS...

....

MOBILE # (Cell)...

HOME #...

WORK #...

FAX...

EMAIL...

NAME..

ADDRESS...

....

MOBILE # (Cell)...

HOME #...

WORK #...

FAX...

EMAIL...

NAME..

ADDRESS...

....

MOBILE # (Cell)...

HOME #...

WORK #...

FAX...

EMAIL...

NOTES:

NAME..

ADDRESS..

....

MOBILE # (Cell)..

HOME #...

WORK #..

FAX...

EMAIL..

NAME..

ADDRESS..

....

MOBILE # (Cell)..

HOME #...

WORK #..

FAX...

EMAIL..

NAME..

ADDRESS..

....

MOBILE # (Cell)..

HOME #...

WORK #..

FAX...

EMAIL..

NOTES:

NAME..

ADDRESS...

....

MOBILE # (Cell)...

HOME #..

WORK #..

FAX..

EMAIL...

NAME..

ADDRESS...

....

MOBILE # (Cell)...

HOME #..

WORK #..

FAX..

EMAIL...

NAME..

ADDRESS...

....

MOBILE # (Cell)...

HOME #..

WORK #..

FAX..

EMAIL...

NOTES:

NAME...

ADDRESS...

....

MOBILE # (Cell)..

HOME #..

WORK #...

FAX...

EMAIL...

NAME...

ADDRESS...

....

MOBILE # (Cell)..

HOME #..

WORK #...

FAX...

EMAIL...

NAME...

ADDRESS...

....

MOBILE # (Cell)..

HOME #..

WORK #...

FAX...

EMAIL...

NOTES:

NAME..

ADDRESS..

....

MOBILE # (Cell)..

HOME #...

WORK #...

FAX...

EMAIL...

NAME..

ADDRESS..

....

MOBILE # (Cell)..

HOME #...

WORK #...

FAX...

EMAIL...

NAME..

ADDRESS..

....

MOBILE # (Cell)..

HOME #...

WORK #...

FAX...

EMAIL...

NOTES:

NAME..

ADDRESS...

....

MOBILE # (Cell)...

HOME #..

WORK #..

FAX..

EMAIL..

NAME..

ADDRESS...

....

MOBILE # (Cell)...

HOME #..

WORK #..

FAX..

EMAIL..

NAME..

ADDRESS...

....

MOBILE # (Cell)...

HOME #..

WORK #..

FAX..

EMAIL..

NOTES:

NAME..

ADDRESS..

....

MOBILE # (Cell)..

HOME #...

WORK #...

FAX..

EMAIL..

NAME..

ADDRESS..

....

MOBILE # (Cell)..

HOME #...

WORK #...

FAX..

EMAIL..

NAME..

ADDRESS..

....

MOBILE # (Cell)..

HOME #...

WORK #...

FAX..

EMAIL..

NOTES:

NAME..

ADDRESS..

....

MOBILE # (Cell)...

HOME #...

WORK #...

FAX...

EMAIL..

NAME..

ADDRESS..

....

MOBILE # (Cell)...

HOME #...

WORK #...

FAX...

EMAIL..

NAME..

ADDRESS..

....

MOBILE # (Cell)...

HOME #...

WORK #...

FAX...

EMAIL..

NOTES:

NAME..
ADDRESS...
....
MOBILE # (Cell)..
HOME #...
WORK #...
FAX...
EMAIL..

NAME..
ADDRESS...
....
MOBILE # (Cell)..
HOME #...
WORK #...
FAX...
EMAIL..

NAME..
ADDRESS...
....
MOBILE # (Cell)..
HOME #...
WORK #...
FAX...
EMAIL..

NOTES:

NAME..

ADDRESS..

....

MOBILE # (Cell)...

HOME #..

WORK #..

FAX...

EMAIL...

NAME..

ADDRESS..

....

MOBILE # (Cell)...

HOME #..

WORK #..

FAX...

EMAIL...

NAME..

ADDRESS..

....

MOBILE # (Cell)...

HOME #..

WORK #..

FAX...

EMAIL...

NOTES:

NAME..
ADDRESS..
....
MOBILE # (Cell)...
HOME #..
WORK #...
FAX..
EMAIL...

NAME..
ADDRESS..
....
MOBILE # (Cell)...
HOME #..
WORK #...
FAX..
EMAIL...

NAME..
ADDRESS..
....
MOBILE # (Cell)...
HOME #..
WORK #...
FAX..
EMAIL...

NOTES:

NAME...
ADDRESS...
....
MOBILE # (Cell)...
HOME #...
WORK #...
FAX..
EMAIL..

NAME...
ADDRESS...
....
MOBILE # (Cell)...
HOME #...
WORK #...
FAX..
EMAIL..

NAME...
ADDRESS...
....
MOBILE # (Cell)...
HOME #...
WORK #...
FAX..
EMAIL..

NOTES:

NAME..

ADDRESS...

....

MOBILE # (Cell)..

HOME #...

WORK #...

FAX..

EMAIL...

NAME..

ADDRESS...

....

MOBILE # (Cell)..

HOME #...

WORK #...

FAX..

EMAIL...

NAME..

ADDRESS...

....

MOBILE # (Cell)..

HOME #...

WORK #...

FAX..

EMAIL...

NOTES:

NAME..

ADDRESS...
....

MOBILE # (Cell)...

HOME #..

WORK #...

FAX..

EMAIL..

NAME..

ADDRESS...
....

MOBILE # (Cell)...

HOME #..

WORK #...

FAX..

EMAIL..

NAME..

ADDRESS...
....

MOBILE # (Cell)...

HOME #..

WORK #...

FAX..

EMAIL..

NOTES:

NAME..

ADDRESS...

....

MOBILE # (Cell)...

HOME #..

WORK #..

FAX..

EMAIL...

NAME..

ADDRESS...

....

MOBILE # (Cell)...

HOME #..

WORK #..

FAX..

EMAIL...

NAME..

ADDRESS...

....

MOBILE # (Cell)...

HOME #..

WORK #..

FAX..

EMAIL...

NOTES:

NAME..

ADDRESS..

....

MOBILE # (Cell)..

HOME #...

WORK #...

FAX...

EMAIL..

NAME..

ADDRESS..

....

MOBILE # (Cell)..

HOME #...

WORK #...

FAX...

EMAIL..

NAME..

ADDRESS..

....

MOBILE # (Cell)..

HOME #...

WORK #...

FAX...

EMAIL..

NOTES:

NAME..

ADDRESS..

....

MOBILE # (Cell)...

HOME #...

WORK #...

FAX..

EMAIL..

NAME..

ADDRESS..

....

MOBILE # (Cell)...

HOME #...

WORK #...

FAX..

EMAIL..

NAME..

ADDRESS..

....

MOBILE # (Cell)...

HOME #...

WORK #...

FAX..

EMAIL..

NOTES:

NAME………………………………………………………………………

ADDRESS………………………………………………………………....

………………………………………………………………………………....

MOBILE # (Cell)………………………………………………..…..

HOME #…………………………………………………………...…....

WORK #…………………………………………………………..........

FAX…………………………………………………………………..

EMAIL……………………………………………………………..

NAME………………………………………………………………………

ADDRESS………………………………………………………………....

………………………………………………………………………………....

MOBILE # (Cell)………………………………………………..…..

HOME #…………………………………………………………...…....

WORK #…………………………………………………………..........

FAX…………………………………………………………………..

EMAIL……………………………………………………………..

NAME………………………………………………………………………

ADDRESS………………………………………………………………....

………………………………………………………………………………....

MOBILE # (Cell)………………………………………………..…..

HOME #…………………………………………………………...…....

WORK #…………………………………………………………..........

FAX…………………………………………………………………..

EMAIL……………………………………………………………..

NOTES:

NAME..
ADDRESS...
....
MOBILE # (Cell)...
HOME #..
WORK #...
FAX...
EMAIL...

NAME..
ADDRESS...
....
MOBILE # (Cell)...
HOME #..
WORK #...
FAX...
EMAIL...

NAME..
ADDRESS...
....
MOBILE # (Cell)...
HOME #..
WORK #...
FAX...
EMAIL...

NOTES:

NAME...

ADDRESS...

....

MOBILE # (Cell)...

HOME #..

WORK #..

FAX..

EMAIL...

NAME...

ADDRESS...

....

MOBILE # (Cell)...

HOME #..

WORK #..

FAX..

EMAIL...

NAME...

ADDRESS...

....

MOBILE # (Cell)...

HOME #..

WORK #..

FAX..

EMAIL...

NOTES:

NAME..

ADDRESS...

....

MOBILE # (Cell)..

HOME #...

WORK #...

FAX..

EMAIL..

NAME..

ADDRESS...

....

MOBILE # (Cell)..

HOME #...

WORK #...

FAX..

EMAIL..

NAME..

ADDRESS...

....

MOBILE # (Cell)..

HOME #...

WORK #...

FAX..

EMAIL..

NOTES:

NAME..

ADDRESS...

....

MOBILE # (Cell)..

HOME #...

WORK #...

FAX..

EMAIL..

NAME..

ADDRESS...

....

MOBILE # (Cell)..

HOME #...

WORK #...

FAX..

EMAIL..

NAME..

ADDRESS...

....

MOBILE # (Cell)..

HOME #...

WORK #...

FAX..

EMAIL..

NOTES:

NAME..

ADDRESS..

....

MOBILE # (Cell)..

HOME #..

WORK #..

FAX..

EMAIL..

NAME..

ADDRESS..

....

MOBILE # (Cell)..

HOME #..

WORK #..

FAX..

EMAIL..

NAME..

ADDRESS..

....

MOBILE # (Cell)..

HOME #..

WORK #..

FAX..

EMAIL..

NOTES:

NAME...

ADDRESS..

....

MOBILE # (Cell)...

HOME #..

WORK #...

FAX...

EMAIL...

NAME...

ADDRESS..

....

MOBILE # (Cell)...

HOME #..

WORK #...

FAX...

EMAIL...

NAME...

ADDRESS..

....

MOBILE # (Cell)...

HOME #..

WORK #...

FAX...

EMAIL...

NOTES:

NAME..

ADDRESS...

....

MOBILE # (Cell)...

HOME #...

WORK #...

FAX..

EMAIL..

NAME..

ADDRESS...

....

MOBILE # (Cell)...

HOME #...

WORK #...

FAX..

EMAIL..

NAME..

ADDRESS...

....

MOBILE # (Cell)...

HOME #...

WORK #...

FAX..

EMAIL..

NOTES:

NAME..

ADDRESS...

....

MOBILE # (Cell)..

HOME #..

WORK #..

FAX...

EMAIL..

NAME..

ADDRESS...

....

MOBILE # (Cell)..

HOME #..

WORK #..

FAX...

EMAIL..

NAME..

ADDRESS...

....

MOBILE # (Cell)..

HOME #..

WORK #..

FAX...

EMAIL..

NOTES:

NAME...

ADDRESS..

....

MOBILE # (Cell)..

HOME #...

WORK #...

FAX...

EMAIL..

NAME...

ADDRESS..

....

MOBILE # (Cell)..

HOME #...

WORK #...

FAX...

EMAIL..

NAME...

ADDRESS..

....

MOBILE # (Cell)..

HOME #...

WORK #...

FAX...

EMAIL..

NOTES:

NAME...
ADDRESS..
....
MOBILE # (Cell)..
HOME #..
WORK #..
FAX...
EMAIL...

NAME...
ADDRESS..
....
MOBILE # (Cell)..
HOME #..
WORK #..
FAX...
EMAIL...

NAME...
ADDRESS..
....
MOBILE # (Cell)..
HOME #..
WORK #..
FAX...
EMAIL...

NOTES:

NAME..

ADDRESS...

....

MOBILE # (Cell)...

HOME #...

WORK #...

FAX...

EMAIL...

NAME..

ADDRESS...

....

MOBILE # (Cell)...

HOME #...

WORK #...

FAX...

EMAIL...

NAME..

ADDRESS...

....

MOBILE # (Cell)...

HOME #...

WORK #...

FAX...

EMAIL...

NOTES:

NAME..
ADDRESS...
....
MOBILE # (Cell)..
HOME #...
WORK #..
FAX..
EMAIL...

NAME..
ADDRESS...
....
MOBILE # (Cell)..
HOME #...
WORK #..
FAX..
EMAIL...

NAME..
ADDRESS...
....
MOBILE # (Cell)..
HOME #...
WORK #..
FAX..
EMAIL...

NOTES:

NAME..

ADDRESS..

....

MOBILE # (Cell)..

HOME #..

WORK #..

FAX..

EMAIL..

NAME..

ADDRESS..

....

MOBILE # (Cell)..

HOME #..

WORK #..

FAX..

EMAIL..

NAME..

ADDRESS..

....

MOBILE # (Cell)..

HOME #..

WORK #..

FAX..

EMAIL..

NOTES:

NAME...

ADDRESS...

....

MOBILE # (Cell)..

HOME #...

WORK #...

FAX..

EMAIL...

NAME...

ADDRESS...

....

MOBILE # (Cell)..

HOME #...

WORK #...

FAX..

EMAIL...

NAME...

ADDRESS...

....

MOBILE # (Cell)..

HOME #...

WORK #...

FAX..

EMAIL...

NOTES: